Your Witness Success

5 Simple Rules For You To Give Good Evidence In A Court Of Law

By Court Counsel

COURT COUNSEL

Your Witness Success

5 Simple Rules For You To Give Good Evidence In A Court Of Law

By Court Counsel

Copyright Notice

This work is dedicated to the spirit of justice, who daily inspires practising legal professionals around the world

Table of Contents

Foreword: The truth, the whole truth, and nothing but the truth

"The truth, the whole truth, and nothing but the truth" are words of a well-used invocation you have heard before, the words of the time-honoured and widely known oath of a witness who is about to tell the judge, the jury, the lawyers and the parties and other people in Court what the witness knows to be true to the best of one's recollection, without favour, without fear, in earnest respect of the service of Justice.

This is serious. You probably know, intentionally giving false evidence can lead to a criminal charge for perjury, which subject is discussed later in this book. Perjury is a rare event. By far, most people do their honest best when giving their evidence. The fact that we are sometimes mistaken in our recollection is no crime. That is human.

So, we conceivably agree, you ought to know what you are doing when you are giving evidence in Court, and in preparation beforehand, especially when the outcome of the case may result in substantial advantage, or disadvantage, to another person, acquainted with you, or not.

Usually, the lawyer in your case will talk to you about the case in conference some time before the Court-appointed hearing date. The lawyer will ask you about what things about the case you know. There may be request for documents. The lawyer will probably give you guidance or tips, like these. The lawyer may suggest you focus your recollection on certain events, actions. The lawyer will take notes or otherwise record the conference.

Nobody is perfect in their recollection.

We are human. We may pause, or stumble in our verbal expression of our recollections of which we may have been confident in what we think we know of the past. But that is before those recollections have been subjected to professional forensic dissection. Ascertainment of the incidents of events we may have seen many years ago, or even last week, may be imprecise in some respects but unshakeable in other respects.

Your steady guidance throughout your acting as a witness in Court must be your serious and publicly expressed personal undertaking of truthfulness.

Should I swear an oath or make an affirmation?

The Court, via the judge or a sheriff or bailiff or other Court officer, will ask you whether you wish to express your undertaking to tell the truth by swearing on the Bible (or the Quran or other holy book) depending on your faith, or a non-religious affirmation.

The Court officer will read aloud to you the words you will be prompted to repeat to make your oath of truthfulness.

If you prefer to make a non-religious profession of your earnest commitment to tell the truth in your evidence, then the Court will accept an affirmation in the form of words that the Court officer will read to you, in the same manner as the oath is administered.

The Court will not be more impressed by you making an oath on the Bible as compared to making an affirmation. The Court is seasoned by years of experience in distinguishing reliable from unreliable evidence.

The purpose of the oath is to fix in the mind of the witness that the evidence to be given is in utmost serious circumstances, and that there are strict penalties for intentionally failing to meet the obligations imposed by the oath and undertaken by the sworn witness.

Evidence: what it is, and why is it needed

In law, a Court decides a case based on facts proved by evidence. What you, as a witness, say to the Court is evidence. What you say in words in your description of past events has the content of facts upon which facts in application of the law the Court will decide the case. Your words, on serious undertaking to tell the truth publicly, may determine the outcome of the case with which you are concerned.

Appearing in Court is a usual thing for many lawyers. Some lawyers never or rarely go to Court, being concerned instead with contracts and matters of that nature. Trial lawyers have seen many cases, judges, and witnesses.

To the lawyer, any case has several necessary requirements (elements) to be met by the facts proved by the evidence.

In a murder case, for instance, against the defendant or accused, the prosecution must prove the following elements:

1. that a human being has been killed ("the body"),

2. that the accused caused that death ("causation"),

3. that the accused was thinking that the victim would die ("intent", "mens rea", "advertence"), and

10

4. that the accused had no good excuse for the intended action causing the death.

Evidence of facts may be spoken ("oral"), or it may be in writing or audio taped or filmed ("documentary evidence"), or "real" evidence, such as a bloodstained knife or a burglar's crowbar.

Documents and real evidence are "tendered" or offered as evidence to the Court by counsel (the lawyers for a party who stand to speak to the judge and jury).

Whether the offered evidence is "admitted" is up to the judge. At the tender, if opposing counsel says "Objection", the judge will ask that lawyer why there is objection. The other counsel may argue against the objection. Just because evidence is admitted onto the Court's record, does not mean it will be accepted in the verdict or the judgment, after closing submissions.

How To Use These 5 Rules

Use the rules to put aside your mind's naturally occurring, possibly insistent, imagination in anticipation of the answers you give in evidence.

It is practically useless to predict which questions counsel will put to you in Court. That is because every Court hearing is necessarily different, and if only to the slightest degree. Any questions you might imagine you might be asked are unlikely to be the questions which are posed to you in Court.

And even if the question you imagine is the question in fact asked of you in Court, if you have rehearsed your answering, those answers will come across or appear as wooden or, well, rehearsed. You are obliged to the Court to give your answer at that time, not something prepared, except in respect of affidavits and written statements and reading from notes.

If the question put in fact is different from your imagining, that may unsettle your prepared answer. You are guided by the lawyers who are calling you to give evidence.

But you will avoid vexation and other worry if you remind yourself to run through these 5 Rules, instead of fervid imaginings of what will transpire in Court. In the time you have before you have to give evidence, practise these 5 Rules.

Use your right hand. Count off the rules.

Hold up your right thumb, then say aloud: "Rule Number 1 is to listen to the words of the question". Then, touch your right index finger, and say to yourself out loud, "Rule Number 2 is to think about the words of the question".

Next, hold up your right middle finger, and say to yourself, "Rule Number 3 is, if the question allows, answer simply Yes or No".

Now use your right ring finger, and say, "Rule Number 4 is, if the question cannot be truthfully answered yes or no, keep the answer short".

Finally, with your right little finger, say "Rule Number 5 is if the truth is 'I don't know' or 'I don't remember', then that is your answer".

Rule 1: Listen to the *words* of the question

Rule 1 is "**Listen** to the **words** of the question".

It is the <u>words</u> of a question, and the <u>words</u> of your answer which are evidence before the Court. There are other forms of evidence, as seen earlier, but the words are the backbone of the case.

Not in evidence is the facial expression of the counsel asking you the question, nor the tone of voice of the questioner. Only the words of the question and the words of the answer go on to the record upon which the judge determines the outcome of the case.

A judge will not permit an advocate to harangue a witness. But a degree of rigor and heat should not surprise, nor intimidate. Counsel may be attempting a strategy of quick, insistent questions. But it is your good right to take your time to listen to and consider the words of the question without being distracted of mixed emotions aroused by an aggressive counsel.

In giving your evidence, you do not want to appear guarded or evasive. Naturally, you want to appear to be respectful, helpful to the best of your ability, and responsive to your obligations in carrying out your part in the process of the law.

Everyone in the court will respect that you are sufficiently attentive to the proceedings to take a half a second to listen to hear the actual words of the question which has been put to you in the witness box.

But it is very important that you respond to the question being asked as well as you can. Again, the question being asked is what meaning is conveyed by the examiner's words in the question.

Have this rule as your practical touchstone when you ready yourself to give evidence.

Let us repeat Rule 1: **Listen** to the **words** of the question.

So be undistracted by whatever you might perceive as the mood of the court room, or the mood of the judge, or the mood of the counsel asking the question, whether it be in chief or in cross examination or whether the judge is asking you a question directly. Be undistracted by what other people in the courtroom are doing. Be undistracted by their looks and facial expressions. What is required of you is the discipline that you bring with these 5 Rules to the job you have to do.

Rule 2: *Think* about the *words* of the question

Rule 2 is: **Think** about the **words** of the question you are being asked.

That is, *pause* before you commence your answer, and think about what you have actually been asked.

You have obliged Rule 1. You have listened to the words of the question. As you listen to the words of the question, you will be in the territory of Rule 2, that is you are already thinking about the words of the question. That focus will sharpen your application of your discipline while giving evidence.

Wwhen you are preparing to give evidence in days perhaps weeks prior to your appearance in court, Rule 1 may be in your thumb, that is, you **listen** to the words of the question, and this Rule 2, to think about the **words** of the question, is your index finger.

These are simple and straight forward disciplines for you to follow.

These rules are only about to make it easier for you to give evidence. You are obliged on your oath to tell the truth as well as you may.

These rules are not at all about allowing you the vanity of imagining that you might tailor your evidence to suit some ulterior purpose. You are sworn to tell the truth. These rules are of the single purpose to make it easier for you to tell the truth.

The purpose or why we **listen** to the words of the question, then pause to **think** about the words of the question before we answer, is to permit us to perform our sworn duty as a witness.

Rule 3: If the *words* of the question allow, simply answer "Yes" or "No"

Rule 3 is - having listened to the words of the question (Rule 1) and thought about the words of the question (Rule 2), whether the question can be answered fully, responsibly, with "yes" or "no" should already be in your mind.

If the question is something like, "Were you at the mall on Saturday?" and the answer truthfully is "yes", that should be your answer.

Do not attempt to add to the answer. It is unnecessary for you to add "… but only for a short time", or "I wanted to get a milkshake", or "I was only there for a minute".

If it becomes a question of "what time were you at the mall", then the counsel or the judge will ask you. If something happened at the mall at 3pm, and you were at the mall at 10am, your answer to the question "Were you at the mall?", is still "Yes".

Counsel will further ask you, "About what time were you at the mall?"

Then you can say, for instance, "About 10.00am for 15 minutes". See Rule 4.

Sometimes counsel pose a "rolled up" question, which is to put forward in the question several different facts. If you cannot affirm the several different pacts postulated, your answer should be "No".

Rule 4: If you cannot answer just "Yes" or "No", keep your answer short

Rule 4 is "If the question cannot be answered yes or no, keep your answer **short**".

For example, if the question is, "What is the weather like today?", and it is fair to describe the day's weather as "humid, overcast, and fine", use just one of those truthful answers. If the day is sunny and hot, your answer should be "sunny" or "hot", not "sunny and hot".

If the question is "What were you doing at the mall?" your answer might be "Meeting a friend" or "Window shopping", or "Drinking a coffee".

In this way you can see you are being responsive to the words of the question and you are telling the truth to the best of your ability, as is your duty under oath. But you are not giving away unnecessary information. If counsel wants more, make the counsel work to frame another question.

Just as it is your job while giving evidence in court to answer truthfully and precisely, it is the job of counsel to frame their every question so that it elicits evidence from the witness, you, which evidence is relevant to the question before the court.

You are not obliged to give your opinion in response to any question. Generally, opinion evidence is only allowed from experts in a field of learning which is outside the normal course of human experience, and in which specialised field, the expert witness has appropriate training and experience. While some expert witnesses will find these 5 Rules useful in their practice of forensic expertise, you should be reluctant to give the court any answer about something you do not know for a fact.

Remembering that we are not in a circumstance of social conversation but in a court of law where serious matters are for determination, then if counsel asks you, for instance, "Was he driving too quickly?" your responsive answer may be "I thought he was driving quickly". To that question there would probably be objection from opposing counsel, or from the judge, because the question is seeking an answer from an expert witness to a fact which is determinative of a central question in the case. On the other hand, given that the question could be answered by resort to rule number 3 (yes or no) you, having listened to the words of the question and thought about the words of the question, are quite entitled to answer with yes or no.

But if the question is more open ended, such as "What were the driving conditions?", you can answer entirely sufficiently with "Fine".

If it is your counsel asking the questions, if your counsel wants more evidence from you on that point, your counsel will ask you further. If it is opposing counsel, then do not be afraid to require that counsel to do their job by asking questions which are simple and straight forward to answer with relevant evidence.

Rule 5: If the truth is you don't know, answer with "I don't know"

Rule 5 is: If it is the truth, you may answer by saying "I don't know", "I don't remember" or "I don't understand the question".

This is an important rule. It is not an excuse to avoid answering questions or to avoid giving evidence. You are bound by your oath to tell the truth. You should meet your obligation to the best of your ability.

It is a forensic resort of, particularly, opposing counsel, to seek to obtain evidence by leaving a question hanging. It is a resort of counsel to ask a question of vague criteria. These resorts are professional devices of seeking to obtain from you spoken words which may be damaging to your party's case. If counsel inveigles you to speak much about which you do not know, then it will be available to counsel to submit that your evidence in other respects is also without the virtue of honest expression.

If counsel puts a question which is complex in that it asks for an answer over inconsistent facts, that will bring to bear Rule 5 which is "If the truth is, I don't know, or I don't remember", then that should be your answer. You can also say you do not understand the question. Counsel will explain the proposition behind a question.

You may not use this rule to attempt to cloak what you know. If the fact is you do not want to give evidence, then tell your counsel or tell the judge. If you do not want to tell the truth, do not take an oath to tell the truth.

"The whole truth" means "only the truth", that is, one should not lie, or make things up, or fib, while giving evidence in Court.

"The whole truth" is not everything you know about something. It is simply that when you tell what you do know, you do not lie. All that you testify must be truthful - "nothing but the truth" – and you do the best you can, by your stating your honest recollection honestly. The oath phrase is a three-part reinforcement of the essential element of truthfulness.

Other matters to think about

- **Before Court, keep quiet**
- **Adopt your poker face**
- **How Court cases proceed**
- **"Objection"**
- **Relevance**
- **Cross examination**
- **Perjury and lying**
- **What should I wear to Court?**

Before Court, keep quiet

You should keep to yourself, and perhaps your spouse, and possibly employer, that you are being called to be a witness in a case. It is nobody else's business. Letting loose with the news may result in harmless gossip only.

But it may be otherwise. For instance, telling of the case in a party setting of any sort, may promote some style of an attack on your credibility in the witness box.

Avoid the risk of that circumstance by keeping to yourself the fact that you will be giving evidence.

Far more serious would be the circumstance of an approach to you, in whatever style, in whichever place or other circumstance, to encourage you either to refrain from being a witness, or by offering inducements or threats with respect to the content of what you intend to testify.

Should that occur, the only thing you can do is inform the lawyer in the case and the police.

Do not tell other people.

Adopt your poker face

That raises another important recommendation for you, which is to keep a "poker face".

Court procedure is serious. You should appear of serious intent. This is not a social occasion.

Whether outside the Court room or within, do not let your face or gestures show your any internal or emotional reaction to other people's conduct of themselves or their evidence or lawyer's submissions or remarks from the judge.

How Court cases proceed

If yours is a jury case, empanelling the jury – "jury selection" – proceeds first. That is often a complicated process but is not for discussion in this outline because it does not involve you as a witness.

If you are acquainted with any people who may be among the jurors, you should not offer any greeting, but you should tell the lawyer for the case in which you are called that you are acquainted with that potential or actual juror.

You should tell the lawyer if you are or have been personally acquainted with witnesses for the other side, the judge or any other Court officer.

After the jury is selected, the way Court cases usually proceed overall is for the prosecution in a criminal case, or the plaintiff in a civil case, to present their case first, then the defendant presents theirs.

Often a judge will ask counsel to "open" by telling the Court what the case is about and outlining the evidence they intend to bring. The judge will often ask the defending counsel to indicate the bases on which the defence is based, and the evidence likely to be brought.

Then the prosecution will call its witnesses, who each give evidence in chief and may be cross-examined. The prosecution will tender reports and other documentary evidence, each of which admitted will be marked as an "exhibit" and allocated an index reference. At simplest, prosecution or plaintiff exhibits will be marked "Exhibit 1" and so on, while those documents and other exhibits for the defence case will be "Exhibit A" and so on.

Not every witness is cross-examined. But some may be questioned in chief or cross-examined for hours, or days. The lawyer in the case in which you are called will let you know when your evidence is likely to be called. There may be delays.

Usually, you will wait outside the Court room before you are called. That is to prevent your evidence being affected or "tainted" by you hearing evidence given by other witnesses. You should not discuss the evidence you are going to give in the case with anyone except the lawyer who is calling you.

A witness who has given their evidence is usually permitted, if they wish, to remain in the public gallery of the Court room to watch the continuing case. Again, in this time, wear your poker face. You are usually entitled to make notes. But in deference to the integrity of the Court proceeding, do not read a book or use your device while sitting in the Court room while the proceedings are continuing. Do not converse with others around you in the Court room. Do not make jokes.

Often there may be "adjournments" of the hearing or trial for any number of reasons, or for any length of time, from several minutes to "standing over" for weeks or months. There may be delays during the hearing while the lawyers attempt to "settle" the case. A witness may not be available at a particular time. Documents may be required to be collected. A person may be ill or otherwise absent. Being patient and calm is a sure guide.

When all the evidence for each side has been admitted and heard, the judge will request counsel for each side to make submissions to the jury or the judge. Sometimes the submissions will be short speeches. Sometimes they may extend for days.

After closing submissions, the judge may give directions or a summary of the case to the jury, and the jury will retire to consider its verdict. When trial by judge alone, the judge may proceed to give judgment in the case by giving reasons as to which evidence is preferred or accepted by reference to the necessary elements of the case.

Often a judge will prefer to adjourn to consider those reasons and will usually have those reasons reduced to writing for presentation to the parties' representatives on another day. The delay may be lengthy because of complexities in the case, or because a judge may be busy with other cases.

When the judgment is delivered, the case is concluded, subject to any party exercising their right by any available avenue of appeal.

"Objection"

Objection may be taken if the question is irrelevant, or if it is a "leading" question, which is when the question suggests an answer, such as "Hot day wasn't it?", although that should be only objectionable if the perceived heat of the day was relevant to proving the existence of one of the necessary elements of the case to be made.

There are many other types of objections to questions or answers of witnesses, such as hearsay (second-hand information), or unresponsiveness, or unqualified opinion. All these objections, and argument about them between the lawyers and the judge, only concern the lawyers, not the witness.

The witness should maintain composure. You might consider adopting a mood of relaxing with a poker face. You should be attentive to any direction to the witness given by the judge. When speaking to the judge, you say "Your Honour" or "Sir" or "Madam" as whichever appropriate.

When it occurs that you need to speak to counsel while giving evidence, say for clarification of a question (which we consider later in this text), use the honorific "Sir" or "Madam", or the honorific and name of counsel. At all times, be respectful and modest in your every expression, no matter if there is exhibited from any counsel in cross examination any overdone sneers, or other emotions.

There are two types of witness, namely ordinary people, or "lay" witnesses, and "expert" witnesses, such as professionals or officers whose training and

33

experience enable them to express opinions about facts relevant to the case. This work is for lay and expert witnesses.

A witness giving evidence in a case is "called" or may be subject to subpoena to testify by one or the other party. Counsel for the party calling the witness brings forth the evidence of the witness by asking questions. That is evidence "in chief". Then counsel for the other party will "cross examine" the witness. For the lawyer, the purpose of cross examination is to weaken the other party's case, usually by bringing into doubt ("discrediting") the evidence given by the witness.

Relevance

The most common objection is "relevance". Relevant evidence is that which may persuade judge or jury to the reasonable belief of the existence of a fact which proves, or tends to prove, one of the elements of the case. This is more than splitting hairs. You can see the layer upon layer of filters.

That is the purpose of the law of evidence, to guide the direction of action of thought ("ratiocination", "cerebration"), which aims to exclude individual impressions and prejudices, so to allow into the Court only fact-based descriptions which can be reasonably understood as relevant by any sensible person whether, or not, they are involved in the circumstances of the case.

Relevance may ground objection to spoken evidence as well as documents. With oral evidence from the witness box, the terms of the question from counsel will logically be the basis of the answer of the witness. The answer is evidence before the Court, the question a necessary incident of the answer.

Cross examination

Cross-examination is dramatic stuff for movie and TV legal thrillers. It is not so much drama in fact. There can be hours of tedious debate and delays. But cross-examination is a vital part of the "forensic" or Court room process.

For you as a witness, you should not fear an attack on you in cross-examination. The cross-examining counsel may adopt any facial expression or bodily posture or tone of voice – derision, scorn, anger, or warm friendliness – but none of those antics should cause you to deviate from your discipline of the 5 Rules you learn from this text.

The 5 Rules are your sturdy brick house against a hard-blowing wolf.

You are always cool, composed and patient when you give your evidence, in chief or in cross.

Perjury and lying

It is fruitless to seek to attempt to deceive the Court.

The judge and the lawyers have seen every witness who seeks deliberately to mislead the Court. Deliberately seeking to mislead the Court is perjury. A judge will not hesitate to refer to the police or the justice department for criminal sanction of someone who gives false evidence to attempt to mislead the Court. Lying in Court wastes everyone's time, including your own.

Acting in accordance with your oath is your substantial contribution to the law which makes our community safer, more prosperous.

Think about it. A judge sees witnesses cross-examined daily, has been professionally engaged for decades in and about this Court process. The lawyers in the case also are often in Court. They have seen some witnesses left discredited, sometimes prosecuted over false evidence. These intelligent, diligent legal professionals are not for fooling, especially from someone who may be appearing in Court once in their lifetime.

The lawyer in your case is by-and-large obliged, if you are the client, to accept and act upon what you say which may be relevant to the case. The lawyer will give you advice based on what you say are the facts and what others might say and what of the events may be corroborated by documents or video evidence.

As a witness in the case, generally a lawyer will make notes of what you say you will tell in Court and will act on what you say. The lawyer is not allowed to tell you what to say. But you should be glad to be guided about what are relevant facts to relate, and what are not. It may be that having heard what evidence you intend to state, the lawyer in the case may decide not to call you as a witness. There are many different reasons peculiar to the case which influence that decision. It really is only the business of the client.

But if you are called and you have conferred with the lawyer and, often, signed a solemn legally prepared statement and sworn the contents to be true, as you have related to the lawyer in the case who acts on your word by putting this evidence before the Court and to the other side, and perhaps to expert witnesses who may express opinions based on the facts you have expressed.

Preparing the statement, serving it on the other side and filing it onto the Court's official record, none of that means the lawyer believes what you say, especially if you are lying. Truth can be stranger than fiction. But imploring to believe the unlikely truthful is never as overdone as exhortation to believe the likely untruthful.

In Court, uncloaking the witness liar is quietly undertaken, highly regarded professional sport. The other side, commonly say in an insurance case, will have resort to years of experience in testing claims and the incidents of claims, particularly the creditworthiness of witnesses, whether for or against a claim.

The habitual or occasional social or pathological liar has slight prospect of succeeding to deceive against seasoned professionally disciplined application of legal professional forensic technique.

What should I wear to Court?

What we wear to court is important. Court is not a fashion show. Because we want the judge and the jury to be undistracted from the words of the evidence we give, we should avoid decorating ourself in any way but with purpose. We dress plainly.

For a man of any age, wear a white shirt with a collar. Brown or beige trousers, matching jacket if convenient. Dark socks, brown leather shoes. An ordinary business suit, if that is what you are used to wearing.

For women, conservative dark suit, white or light blouse. Minimal jewellery. Simple comfortable shoes. Hair simple, neat, unremarkable. Likewise make up, hardly any. Small, dark handbag, if necessary.

If normally you wear body piercing jewellery or clubber cosmetics, take all that off. Be as plain as possible.

The idea is to appear unnoteworthy but appropriate.

Think about the visual context of the court room. For the judge and the attorneys, court is their daily work. The judge, court clerks and bailiffs or sheriffs, they must dress in robes for a judge, the attorneys nearly always either in robes or a business suit. The court officers will be wearing, as they do every working day, their business suit or their uniform. But they are not going to be called to give evidence as a witness.

As a witness to give evidence, our purpose is to have the judge accept our evidence. As you may appreciate, the judge and the court officers often have morning tea or lunch or afternoon tea in each other's company, and often joined by the attorneys.

Remember the judge and the officers have seen thousands of witnesses giving evidence. Like all people, their tea room conversations will be gossip, that is, the usual workplace conversation exchanges as you know by experience occurs in a coal mine or between farmhands or at the factory or at the office or in the boardroom. As a witness we do not want to be noticed apart from the evidence we give.

We will be noticed if we turn up in court dressed to impress. None of the court officers, including the judge, will afford us respect if we make our appearance dressed to the nines in catwalk designer outfits or gangster-wear. At court as a witness we dress to be utterly unremarkable. That permits others to focus on the words of our evidence, and not be distracted by irrelevant matter.

Of course, if I am being called as a witness in a complicated business case where the evidence I am to give is, say from a bank officer, then I would wear a plain suit and tie. If I am a doctor, similarly I would wear a suit, but not my clinical outfit and stethoscope.

But if I am a witness in a case of drink driving or some domestic dispute and my occupation is not an occupation or position where one would expect me to wear a suit then I should not dress up but rather merely neatly ordinary.

A good rule of thumb is to dress as though you may be attending a christening of the child of a friend. We are neat and tidy but someone else is the star of the show, not us.

Most courts are generally open to the public. If you are going to be a witness in a particular Court, then going to that Court some days ahead of when you will be giving evidence should be useful in this respect. Go to the Court and sit in the back rows of seats and merely observe how the business is conducted. Measure the advice you have just read against your observations of the apparent dress codes.

The Court will respect a person who gives the Court respect. Obtaining the respect of the Court is a vital ingredient of the acceptability of your evidence. Court is nothing like any television drama. The Court does not care two hoots what you think of the legal system. And highly dramatic moments are rare.

After you have given your evidence, the Court will be dealing with another witness. Remember, the Court hears witnesses give evidence day in, day out. The Court is a workplace for its officers. It is not a place for jokes or any type of other attention seeking behaviour.

If you are going to be an effective witness, leave aside any notions of Court room drama or your any homespun notion of how justice should be administered.

If you are honestly and seriously concerned with the administration of justice, your best effective course forward is to obtain a professional qualification and lend your ideal to practice the learning and wisdom of those who have gone before you and are alongside you.

Because the case in which you will be giving evidence as a witness may involve substantial sums of money or a question of imprisonment, you can see that some serious thought and preparation is warranted.

None of this is to suggest to you to attempt to alter your straightforward recollection of events. None of this is to persuade you to be other than yourself. Your evidence needs only to be truthful.

As the 5 Rules teach you, there is no call for you to attempt to achieve some margin of cleverness over the judge or the attorneys who may be asking you questions. Your sworn duty is to tell the truth to the best of your ability. That is the only yard stick you should apply. Your outside world notions of what is right and just must be constrained by your respect for the function of the Court at that moment in that case with which you are concerned.

The message here is clear: what you should wear to Court is a humble and respectful attitude.

Outside Court while you are waiting to give evidence, avoid any conversation with any person apart from Court officers and your party's attorney. That is because you may not know who you are talking to, and just as importantly, who may be listening to your conversation.

With any Court officer, we are always cool, attentive, respectful, even if in the unlikely event the officer is in any way impolite. We address a Court officer as "Sir" or "Ma'am". The same for the judge or, "Your Honour".

About the Author

Court Counsel is the pen name of a well-reputed trial lawyer with decades of experience conducting trials across many fields of law as a prosecutor, defence counsel and acting judge. In private practice, Court Counsel acts for corporations, individuals, public institutions and partnerships.

"The 5 Rules are your sturdy brick house against a hard-blowing wolf."

"A good rule of thumb is to dress as though you may be attending a christening of the child of a friend. We are neat and tidy but someone else is the star of the show, not us."

"Think about the visual context of the court room."

"Talking about the case, in a social party setting of any sort, may promote attack on your credibility in the witness box."

"Professional expert witnesses will find these 5 Rules especially useful in their forensic practice."

Printed in Great Britain
by Amazon

39860161R00026